Love Magic

A Beginner's Guide to
Harnessing Magic for
Love and Romance

Lydia Levine

summersdale

LOVE MAGIC

Copyright © Octopus Publishing Group Limited, 2025

All rights reserved.

Text by Nicola Skinner

No part of this book may be reproduced by any means, nor transmitted, nor translated into a machine language, without the written permission of the publishers.

Condition of Sale
This book is sold subject to the condition that it shall not, by way of trade or otherwise, be lent, resold, hired out or otherwise circulated in any form of binding or cover other than that in which it is published and without a similar condition including this condition being imposed on the subsequent purchaser.

An Hachette UK Company
www.hachette.co.uk

Summersdale Publishers
Part of Octopus Publishing Group Limited
Carmelite House
50 Victoria Embankment
LONDON
EC4Y 0DZ
UK

www.summersdale.com

This FSC® label means that materials and other controlled sources used for the product have been responsibly sourced

The authorized representative in the EEA is Hachette Ireland, 8 Castlecourt Centre, Dublin 15, D15 XTP3, Ireland (email: info@hbgi.ie)

Printed and bound in Poland

ISBN: 978-1-83799-689-6
eISBN: 978-1-83799-690-2

Substantial discounts on bulk quantities of Summersdale books are available to corporations, professional associations and other organizations. For details contact general enquiries: telephone: +44 (0) 1243 771107 or email: enquiries@summersdale.com.

Disclaimer
Neither the author nor the publisher can be held responsible for any injury, loss or claim – be it health, financial or otherwise – arising out of the use, or misuse, of the suggestions made herein.

Contents

4   Introduction

6   A Word of Warning

8   The Basics of Witchcraft

32   The Essentials of Love Magic

56   Spells for Loving Yourself

80   Spells for Finding Love

104   Spells for True Love

128   Spells for Friendship

152   Conclusion

154   Notes

Introduction

Welcome, dear seeker, to the magical world of love spells. Whether this book was given to you by someone special or found its way into your hands by chance, take it as a sign: love is within your reach.

Working with love magic is not about control; it is about beautiful, life-changing shifts. Love magic is intended for both new and experienced witches, because love's energy is obtainable to all those who open their hearts to it.

This type of magic begins within. Before casting spells or setting intentions, take a moment to connect with yourself. True enchantment flows from self-love, self-worth and the belief that you are deserving of the love you seek. When you embrace your own radiance, you naturally attract relationships and experiences that reflect that light back to you. So, let this book be more than just a guide – let it be an awakening to the magic that already exists within your heart.

Finally, bear in mind that this journey is not just about romance; it's about infusing every part of your life with the magic of different kinds of love. It's about stepping into the light of tenderness, passion, devotion and kindness.

This book begins with spells for self-love, helping you embrace your worth and inner light. From there, you'll explore spells for romance, deep connection and friendship – because love takes many forms, and each one is a gift.

You deserve love. So, light a candle, take a deep breath and let your personal love journey begin.

A Word of Warning

When using fire, candles, smudge sticks or water in your love spells, always prioritize safety. Never leave flames unattended, keep safety principles in mind around open water – especially if there are young children or animals nearby – and ensure candles are placed on heat-resistant surfaces. Avoid rushing through rituals – accidents can happen when you're distracted. Always perform spells with a clear mind, when you have plenty of time and can give them your full focus.

If you're using spells to meet new people, ensure your personal safety by meeting them somewhere public, and always tell a friend where you're going.

When it comes to the spells themselves, approach them with care and respect for others. The Wiccan Rede, a guiding principle in magical practice, reminds us to avoid harm to others, ourselves and the world around us. Its core message, *"An it harm none, do what ye will,"* encourages mindfulness, compassion and honouring the free will of others. Love cannot be forced or manufactured; it blooms naturally when it's meant to be. So, rather than trying to influence someone's feelings, use magic to invite love from others, nurture self-love or strengthen bonds that already exist. By respecting free will, you create space for true, meaningful connections.

The Basics of Witchcraft

Welcome to the incredibly rewarding world of witchcraft! This chapter will help you lay the groundwork for your exciting journey through love magic. Explore the core principles and practices that form the heart of the craft and you'll learn about its sacred history, as well as the tools and rituals that will prepare you to work confidently with love magic. You'll also discover how to harness your own energy, aligning your intentions with the universe to manifest true feelings of connection. By the end of this chapter, you'll be ready to begin your journey towards better, stronger, more authentic love.

The chance to love and be loved exists no matter where you are.

OPRAH WINFREY

LOVE FOR ALL LIFE IS WITCHCRAFT'S ESSENCE

What is witchcraft?

Witchcraft is a spiritual practice that centres around harnessing the energies of nature and the universe to manifest change for good. Historically, witches have been healers, diviners and spiritual guides, using their knowledge of herbs, the stars and the elements to bring about wellness and protection.

Witchcraft isn't a religion, but you can incorporate religious or spiritual beliefs into its practices. Modern witchcraft is very diverse, encompassing everything from Wicca to other eclectic and secular practices.

For some, witchcraft involves deities, while others focus more on nature, energy and the elements. Some practitioners follow structured traditions, while others develop highly personal, intuitive approaches that evolve over time. Many witches find empowerment in their craft, using it to cultivate confidence, resilience and a deeper connection with their true selves.

However you choose to practise, all witchcraft requires respect, mindfulness and a willingness to connect with the unseen forces around us. It is also intuitive and as much a process of self-discovery as it is about other people. No two witches are the same, and the beauty of witchcraft lies in the freedom to explore and create a practice that feels authentic to you.

The origins of witchcraft

Long before books, spells were woven into fabric and spirits were invoked. In ancient Egypt, practitioners called upon Hathor, goddess of love, using spells and amulets – some of these are still displayed in the British Museum in London. In Mesopotamia, clay tablets inscribed with love spells and protective incantations were buried beneath homes, while in Greece and Rome, witches crafted love potions and engraved charms dedicated to deities, blending magic with everyday life.

In Celtic traditions, the cycles of nature and the changing seasons shaped magical beliefs. The Druids were said to possess deep knowledge of the natural world, creating herbal remedies and divining the future.

Their sacred stone circles were places of powerful rituals meant to bring protection, love and harmony.

As Christianity spread, witches were unfairly branded as heretics, leading to persecution – yet witchcraft endured. Hidden in folklore and secret traditions, it survived through midwives, herbalists and others who believed in its powers, determined to keep the ancient wisdoms alive.

Today, witchcraft thrives as a modern, diverse practice, blending that inherited wisdom with new ideas. Whether rooted in tradition or innovation, it's always about personal power, natural energies and spiritual connection – an ever-evolving and intensely personal magical path.

The core principles of witchcraft

Witchcraft is a disciplined practice grounded in ethics and strict guidelines:

- The Wiccan Rede encourages acting responsibly and causing no harm through magic.
- Balance is key, aligning with the moon's cycles, seasons and elements to maintain harmony in life and magical practices.
- The Threefold Law, a principle in Wicca whose exact origins are unclear, teaches that the energy you put out – good or bad – returns to you threefold, emphasizing kindness and positivity while warning against harm or negativity.

Like many belief systems, witchcraft values community and respect. By honouring the universe and those within it, you create a strong foundation for your practice.

What's in it for you?

Witchcraft, practised with good intentions, is like unlocking a door to transformation. It taps into your inner strength, aligns your energy and helps bring your desires to life. Plus, it sharpens intuition while boosting confidence and inner peace. It helps you come face to face with your needs and allows you to put them into words.

As for love? It's a game changer. Love magic can nurture self-love, heal emotional wounds and attract meaningful connections. And that's really just scratching the surface. What will it do for you? Turn the pages and let's find out.

Types of witchcraft

Witchcraft is not a one-size-fits-all practice – there are numerous paths to explore, each resonating differently with every practitioner.

- Wicca, one of the most popular traditions, honours the God and Goddess, celebrates the Sabbats (seasonal festivals) and works with lunar cycles to connect with nature and the divine. It also includes rituals focused on the elements, the Wheel of the Year cyclical calendar and celebrating personal spiritual growth.
- Eclectic witchcraft offers freedom by allowing individuals to blend elements from various traditions, including Wicca, folk magic and other spiritual practices. This flexibility empowers practitioners to create a deeply personal and evolving spiritual path, embracing diverse influences and techniques.

- Kitchen witchery focuses on making magic through everyday activities like cooking and homemaking. It emphasizes the energy in simple, domestic tasks, weaving intention into creating a nurturing environment that aligns with magical practices.
- Green witchcraft connects practitioners to the natural world, using plants, herbs and nature's cycles in rituals. This encourages eco-conscious living in harmony with the earth, for healing and growth.
- Traditional witchcraft draws on ancient, regional practices, often passed down through generations, communities and families, blending old-world folklore, ancestral wisdom and regional customs, and creating a practice that is both rooted in history and ever-evolving within contemporary witchcraft.

Today's witch

Anyone with a sincere heart, an open mind and curiosity about the mysteries of the universe can become a witch today. Witchcraft isn't restricted by lineage, age or gender – it's an inclusive and ever-changing practice for those who seek wisdom.

When you practise love magic, you aren't just casting spells for today; you're tapping into a long-held tradition that honours love as a transformative force.

By working with this special force, you join the legacy and collective influence of witches who have celebrated love's sacred power for centuries. From herbalists and midwives to modern spellcasters, witches have always recognized the magic within love. They've taught us that love is the ultimate creative force – a force that transcends time, space and the boundaries of the heart.

So, as you light your candles or speak your intentions, know that you're drawing from this rich lineage. You are part of a timeless tradition where love and magic are intertwined, and your magic has the potential to heal and transform your world. In fact, you could say that believing this is your very first spell.

Ethics

Ethics are central to witchcraft. Personal responsibility, kindness and respect are key principles. Your magic should empower and heal, not control or manipulate others. Interfering with free will is considered unethical.

The Threefold Law, previously mentioned on page 16, explains that the energy you emit into the world around you, whether negative or positive, comes back to you threefold. This highlights the importance of practising with integrity.

Ethical witches focus on healing, protection and manifesting positive outcomes. With good intentions, witchcraft becomes a powerful tool for growth and transformation, bringing positive change to your life and the world around you.

Meditation and grounding

Both of these practices can be really useful in witchcraft, keeping you balanced and in tune with your magic.

Meditation connects you to your inner self, sharpens intuition and focuses energy. It can involve deep breathing, quiet reflection or visualizing a link with elements or deities.

Grounding reconnects you to the earth to release excess energy and restore balance. Simple methods include walking barefoot, leaning against a tree or visualizing roots anchoring you.

Together, these practices clear mental clutter and stabilize energy to keep your magic powerful and effective, creating the foundation of an empowered witchcraft practice.

Finding your tribe

Finding like-minded people in witchcraft can be a rewarding experience, enabling you to share knowledge, grow your practice and connect with individuals you feel an affinity with. There are several ways to meet fellow witches, both in person and online, and you'll find your confidence and skills will grow rapidly within a community.

- Seek out local witchcraft groups, spiritual communities or metaphysical shops. These spaces offer opportunities to learn, connect and grow spiritually with others.
- Look for shops that host events, workshops or classes where you can meet other practitioners, to network, share experiences and deepen your magical knowledge.

- Find groups through social media platforms, like Facebook or Instagram, where local covens or meetups are often advertised. Websites such as meetup.com also offer listings for spiritual or witchcraft-based gatherings. This and other websites are excellent resources for discovering both local and virtual events to expand your practice and circle.
- Attend public events such as full moon circles, sabbat celebrations or occult fairs for opportunities to meet others.
- Join any of the countless forums and discussion boards where you can connect with witches globally, sharing insights and advice.

Witchcraft is a personal practice, but sharing it with others allows you to expand your knowledge, exchange ideas and find a sense of belonging.

Setting intentions

Setting intentions is key to witchcraft. Knowing what you want is the spark that carries your desires into the universe. Here's an easy way to learn how:

- Be specific – what do you truly want? Visualize it vividly, as if it's already happening.
- Write it down or speak it aloud to strengthen its energy.
- Not just about wishes, intentions will help to align your actions with your goals. Rooted in respect and honesty, they reflect what you're ready to pursue.
- In love magic, for instance, intentions around self-love and healing can help create genuine transformation.
- A well-set intention connects your emotions, thoughts and actions, laying the foundation for positive change and manifestation.

Casting spells

Spellcasting is the art of turning your dreams into reality, weaving intention and energy into powerful magic.

- To begin, create a sacred space and call on the elements or deities for guidance.
- Be clear about your intention and focus on what you truly want. Spells are about co-creating with the universe, so energy and focus are your keys to success.
- While casting, visualize your goal, chant or use your chosen tools, such as candles, herbs or crystals, to manifest a specific result.
- Let go of any attachment to the outcome – trust that the universe will bring your desires into being.

Creating your sacred space

A personal sanctuary, sometimes referred to as an altar, serves as a focal point for rituals, meditation and spell work. It's important to have a special space to ground yourself, raise your energy and recharge.

- This space can be as simple as a small table or shelf, or as elaborate as an entire room. The point is that the space feels sacred, inspiring and empowering.
- Many witches decorate their altar with items related to the elements, or to represent their deities or intentions.

- Common altar items include candles, crystals, incense, statues and symbols of nature.
- When you enter this space, you're signalling to yourself and the universe that you are about to enter a realm of intention and magic.
- Remember that altars are highly personal, so have fun when creating yours. It should reflect your practice and your journey, so it's very normal to regularly switch things up. See your altar as a work in progress.

Whether it's for spellcasting, healing or simply grounding, your sacred space is where you align your energies and connect with the divine.

Deities and gods

Deities and gods embody the natural forces, universal energies and personal archetypes that shape our lives. Connecting with a deity for your practice adds depth, focus and inspiration. In witchcraft, practitioners are not limited to a specific set of deities or gods. One of the beautiful aspects of the practice is its flexibility, allowing inspiration to be drawn from a wide variety of cultural, mythological and spiritual sources.

- To find a deity, start by considering what you're drawn to. Is it love, wisdom, creativity or protection? Research myths, symbols and historical practices. Keep an open mind and let intuition guide you to a connection.

- Create a small altar with offerings such as candles, flowers or food to welcome their presence.

- Different deities – from all cultures and mythologies – align with specific energies. Aphrodite, for example, governs love and beauty, while Thor represents strength and protection. Exploring mythology can help you discover gods and goddesses who may be appropriate for your beliefs, needs or personal journey.
- Working with a deity is about forming a respectful partnership. Always approach them with gratitude and sincerity.
- By aligning with a deity, you tap into a vast, ancient source of power and wisdom, enriching your craft and creating a bridge to something greater than yourself. This connection nurtures both your magic and your spirit.

The Essentials of Love Magic

It's time to turn your attention to the essentials of love sorcery. In this chapter, you'll learn the best times, phases of the moon and locations for casting powerful spells. As well as discovering the crucial preparation steps, and the dos and don'ts of ethical magic, you'll learn how to craft powerful affirmations that supercharge your spells – bringing focus and intention to your desires – and understand how long they might take to work. Whether you're hoping to attract new love, deepen a connection or are embracing self-love, these pages will help your magic shine brightly.

What is love magic?

Love magic is a practice that uses focused intention, ritual and symbolic tools to align your energy with the vibrations of love in many forms.

It's not about controlling someone's feelings. Instead, it's about amplifying your desires and inviting love to flow into your life naturally. Magic in this context works by focusing your will and intention on the type of love you want to manifest.

When practising love magic, it's essential to stay true to yourself and ensure that the intentions you set align with your best self. Ultimately, love magic isn't about force – it's about creating the space for love to grow and bloom naturally.

Cultivating confidence

The foundation of successful love magic starts within you. Before attracting or nurturing love with others, you must first tend to your own sense of worth. Try these practices if you need a boost:

- Incorporate rituals that lift your confidence into your daily routine, such as standing tall in front of a mirror, repeating empowering affirmations.
- Practise daily gratitude for the qualities that make you unique. Notice when you are kind, strong and imaginative, and take time to appreciate your actions and deeds.

By prioritizing your own confidence and self-worth, you align yourself with the energy of healthy, fulfilling love.

Finding time and place

Where you perform love magic can greatly impact your success. You will need a space that's calm, free from distractions and cleared of negative energy. Many witches choose to create an altar. This can be simple and personal; it doesn't need to be elaborate – setting up a candle on your desk or putting a crystal in a quiet corner can work beautifully. The most important thing is to find a place where you can connect deeply with your intention and feel grounded in your power.

If you want the potency of ritual and atmosphere, casting under the moonlight or outdoors can amplify your power and belief. The waxing moon is perfect for attracting love, while the full moon radiates power for manifestation. Some practitioners also align their magic with planetary hours for extra potency. Ultimately, the right time is when you feel most focused and connected, and confident in remaining undisturbed by the demands of a busy life. Listen to your inner rhythm – whether it's at sunrise, sunset or in the quiet of night.

Wherever and whenever you choose, ensure the space is peaceful. Cleanse it with sage or incense to remove stagnant energy.

How fast do love spells work?

You might be wondering how quickly love spells take to set in and when you'll see results. The truth is, they rarely yield instant outcomes – and they're stronger for it. Patience, and trust in the process, are essential. These spells take time to manifest, depending on factors such as the complexity of the spell, your intentions and the energy you've invested in it. Try to see the time as a chance to regularly check in with yourself and your reasons for searching for this particular kind of love.

To feel more in tune with the process throughout, try keeping a journal to document your emotions, experiences and any subtle shifts you notice. Writing down your observations can help you stay connected to the energy you've set in motion and provide clarity about the changes occurring around you.

It's also helpful to reflect on and appreciate small signs of progress. Synchronicities, dreams, things falling into place or a sudden sense of peace can be signs your spell is working. Practising mindfulness or meditating on your intentions can reinforce the positive energy you've released. Be open to how love enters your life – it might not align perfectly with your initial expectations but could bring unexpected blessings. And remember, your patience will be rewarded.

The role of affirmations

Affirmations are statements of personal belief imbued with intention. In love magic, they are a potent tool for reinforcing spells and opening your heart to worthiness. An affirmation such as "Love flows effortlessly into my life" can clarify and amplify your magical work, while reshaping your inner dialogue to embody the energy you wish to attract.

Though today's affirmations may feel contemporary, their roots lie deep in mystical traditions that understood the power of intentional repetition to shape existence.

To uncover pronouncements that resonate, reflect on what you truly seek in love – self-love, connection or healing. Let your intuition guide you. Keep the affirmations positive, focused on the present and brimming with belief. Whisper them in meditation, write them in your journal or chant them during rituals. If you're crafty, why not incorporate them into a piece of art or embroidery?

For deeper focus, choose one or two at a time and infuse them with your trust.

Here are some examples to give you an idea:

- Love flows effortlessly into my life.
- I am worthy of deep, fulfilling love.
- My heart is open to giving and receiving love.
- I create love in my life through kindness and intention.
- The universe aligns to bring me loving connections.

Know the risks

Magic is a potent force that responds to your energy and intentions, and like all powerful forces, it's good to know what the risks are. This will help you approach magic with a sense of respect and awareness. Remember, it's only human to feel negative emotions. The universe will notice and repay you when you don't act on them.

The temptation to manipulate another person's feelings

Attempting to control someone's emotions may disrupt the natural flow of energy and lead to unintended negative consequences.

Approaching magic from a place of need or desperation

When we cast spells in this way, it can reinforce feelings of insecurity or unworthiness. It's important to cultivate healthy self-love and emotional balance first, before inviting genuine love into our lives.

Knowing these risks from the outset means you can approach your practice with clarity and confidence. It's not about fearing the magic, but understanding the responsibility that comes with it. When you approach love magic with pure intentions, the universe will respond in kind, bringing the love that is truly meant for you.

Dos and don'ts

Love magic is most effective when practised within boundaries. Aligning your energy with positive desires ensures your spells manifest harmoniously. Keep these key dos and don'ts in mind for ethical, successful results:

- **Do** approach love magic with a pure heart. Your intentions should come from a place of love, rather than negativity or ill will. Remember that the energy you send out will be reflected back to you.

- **Do** be realistic with your desires. While magic can open doors, it's important to be mindful of what is truly possible. Love magic should enhance, rather than replace, genuine effort in building healthy relationships.

- **Do** take responsibility for your actions. Love magic isn't a quick fix, but a tool to guide you towards the love you deserve.
- **Don't** rush. Trust that the universe will work in its own time. Love magic shouldn't be hurried, so allow space for things to unfold naturally.
- **Don't** cast spells out of anger or frustration. Negative emotions can lead to unpredictable results, so always approach love magic from a place of calm and positivity.
- **Don't** neglect your personal energy. Regular self-care helps maintain the flow of love magic in your life.

The privilege of a lifetime is to become who you truly are.

CARL JUNG

Herbs and plants

Botanical allies have been used in love magic for centuries because of their unique energies. Here are some to get you started:

- Roses are perfect for self-love and romantic spells. Sprinkle petals into a bath to invite love into your life.
- Lavender promotes harmony and emotional balance – ideal for healing or strengthening existing relationships.
- Cinnamon ignites passion and adds fiery energy to love rituals.
- Basil is associated with protection and attraction. Carry it in your pocket or place it under your pillow to attract love.

Use these herbs, flowers and spices in teas, baths or spells, and grow roses, lavender or basil at home to create a constant source of love energy.

Your spells kit

While you don't need an elaborate set-up, certain artefacts carry potent symbolism and can enhance the flow of your magic. These tools help focus your intention, amplify your energy and deepen your connection to your spellwork:

- Candles are a sacred choice – pink for love, red for passion or white for purity and spiritual connection. Lighting a candle is a simple yet powerful ritual that sheds light on your intentions.
- Rose quartz, a vessel of heart-healing energy, is another essential ally in love magic. Holding it or placing it in your space can help open your heart to love and compassion.

- Herbs and flowers – such as rosemary, lavender and rose petals – are often used for their loving energy, whether in a spell or burned as incense to fill your space with their fragrant magic.
- You can also work with charms, amulets and oils, each designed to carry your intention wherever you go.

Experiment with different mystical implements to see what resonates with you. Browse shops and stalls or explore nature, and let your intuition guide you to the artefacts that will support your unique journey of love magic.

How to cast a spell

1 Begin by creating a serene, sacred space – a clean room, a quiet corner or even a cosy nook outdoors. Ensure this space feels safe, comfortable and free of distractions. You may also want to add flowers, symbols or written affirmations to enhance the energy of your thoughts and work. Clear the space and your mind by burning sage or incense, ringing a bell, visualizing white light or simply taking a few deep, calming breaths.

2 Light a candle (pink or red work well) to symbolize the spark of love, and use a crystal such as rose quartz to amplify your intention.

3. Now, focus your energy on the love you wish to attract. Visualize it vividly, imagining the warmth, joy and connection it brings. Allow yourself to feel as if it is already present in your life.

4. Speak a heartfelt mantra or chant appropriate to the spell, releasing it like whispers to the universe. Let your emotions rise, filling the space with your passion and belief.

5. Let go of your spell with trust, knowing the universe is already working its wonders. Magic thrives on faith – believe in the love you seek and watch as it finds its way to you.

Taking it online

You can use your phone and other tech to practise love magic. This might be useful if you work in shared spaces without access to the sacred privacy you might have at home.

Digital sigils – symbols imbued with intention and created to manifest a specific desire – can be drawn on smartphones or tablets using design apps like Canva or specific sigil apps that you find in your app store. To create a sigil, design a unique symbol that represents your goal, such as love or self-worth, and visualize its energy as you draw. Set it as your wallpaper or store it on your device to carry the magic with you.

Technology can also enhance your magical timing and intention. Apps that track moon phases can help you plan spells for optimal results, while writing affirmations in notes apps creates virtual talismans.

Incorporate platforms you already use. Post love-themed affirmations or gratitude lists on social media, or use journalling apps to focus on self-love rituals. Even sending texts filled with heartfelt energy to loved ones can channel magical intention.

By blending ancient wisdom with modern innovation, love magic adapts beautifully to contemporary lifestyles, offering endless creative possibilities to infuse magic into everyday life.

Bringing love magic into the everyday

Love magic thrives on creativity and intention. One delicious way to experiment is through baking – a simple, spiced vanilla cake, for example, can become a powerful spell. Vanilla draws love and comfort, cinnamon sparks passion and nutmeg encourages luck in relationships.

If art calls to you, paint or draw your vision of love. Imagine the warmth of an embrace or the joy of shared laughter, and channel those feelings into your creation.

Music can also be a powerful tool – compose a melody, hum a tune or build a playlist that vibrates with loving energy, sending your intentions out into the universe.

Experiment, play and let your interests become part of your practice.

Love magic at a glance

Love magic is a personal and evolving practice that blends tradition with creativity. As you explore the following chapters, keep these six tips in mind:

1 Intent is key: Focus your energy and set clear goals for your magic.

2 Start with self-love: Build self-respect as a foundation for all love magic.

3 Respect boundaries: Practise ethically, honouring consent and free will.

4 Make magic part of your life: Turn simple actions, like journalling or listening to music, into powerful rituals.

5 Go at your own pace: Decide what works for you.

6 Remember it's a process: Enjoy the exploration.

Ready to begin?

Spells for Loving Yourself

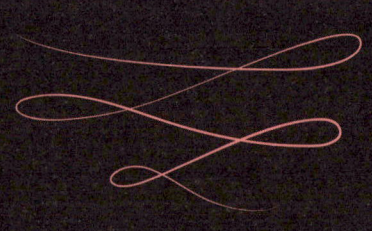

Remember, love starts with you and to fully embrace it in its truest form you must first focus on yourself. This chapter offers spells, rituals and potions to help you grow your self-love and thrive as a unique individual.

Follow your intuition and dip in as you wish, or work through the spells and rituals sequentially – they are thoughtfully arranged to build self-love using a gentle, gradual process, layer by layer.

While you work on your self-love, you may occasionally come face to face with challenging memories or thought patterns. Let these all come out and be sure to treat yourself with kindness. You deserve it.

Love yourself first and everything else falls into line.

LUCILLE BALL

Building an altar

It's important to have a sacred space dedicated to your practice.

On a small table, shelf or tray, gather personal items that represent your best qualities and happiest times. Arrange a candle and crystal, or another object of your choice, that speaks to you.

Arrange your chosen items on the altar and place your crystal or object at the centre to anchor the space in its empowering energy.

Light the candle and, as it burns, honour yourself with a mantra or affirmation. Feel love healing and rebuilding you. You can practise spells here, or alternatively just spend regular time in quiet contemplation and reflection to support yourself.

A spell to acknowledge yourself now

Recognizing and validating your emotions is the first step in understanding your needs and embracing your true self. This simple spell helps you connect with this powerful side of you. See every emotion, even the difficult or tricky ones, as a gateway to your strength. Each feeling is not an obstacle but a guide, offering wisdom to deepen your self-awareness. By honouring and accepting each emotion as it arises, you open yourself up to greater emotional clarity and growth. With this spell, you align with your inner wisdom, learning to trust and navigate the complexities of your heart.

You will need:

- Blue candle
- Bowl of water
- Piece of paper
- Pen

Casting the spell:

- Light the blue candle, symbolizing clarity.
- Write your emotions on the paper in words or phrases that resonate with you. These may be feelings you've had for some time or recent ones. All are valid.

- Place the paper in the water, let the ink blur, and say: "I honour my feelings, for they will show me the way." Spend a moment acknowledging that your feelings will guide you towards the answers you seek.
- Pour the water outdoors, somewhere special if possible, allowing your emotions – both negative and positive – to flow freely.

Potion for healthy boundaries

Boundaries are a vital early step in self-love because they safeguard your energy, enabling you to build a strong foundation for further emotional healing and empowerment. By sprinkling this potion around yourself, you'll create a safe space for love to grow.

In this potion, sea salt is a purifier of energy, establishing a sacred boundary to shield you from external negativity; rosemary is associated with clarity and strength, helping you to assert your boundaries with confidence and resilience; and lavender has calming and grounding properties to keep you centred and serene, while reinforcing emotional protection.

You will need:
- 1 tsp of sea salt
- Sprig of rosemary
- Sprig of lavender
- Bowl
- Jar

Brewing the potion:
- Combine your ingredients in a bowl. As you blend them, feel the energy growing stronger, creating a protective aura around you. Visualize a radiant shield of light surrounding you in your space.
- Sprinkle the mixture around yourself slowly, and with intent, saying: "This is my sacred space, where

only healthy love and respect may enter. Nothing else shall pass." Repeat this phrase a few times in a firm strong voice that grows louder each time.
- Store the remaining mixture in a jar and use whenever you need it. Have faith that it will continue to protect and empower you.

Forgiveness spell

Compassion is a cornerstone of self-love. You can use it to create space in your life to move on. This spell helps you release the weight of the past, by forgiving yourself or someone else.

In this spell, the white candle represents renewal and purity, the water is for cleansing, the salt is for protection and purification, and the basil or pebble is for healing and grounding.

You will need:

- White candle
- Bowl of water
- Pinch of salt
- Basil leaf or smooth pebble

Casting the spell:

- Light the white candle to welcome clarity and a fresh start. Place the basil leaf or pebble by the bowl.
- Hold the bowl of water in your hands and sprinkle in the salt, imagining it washing away the past.
- Gently swirl the water. Focus on the mistake or memory you want to let go of.
- Dip your fingers into the water, touch your heart and feel forgiveness flowing through you.

- Pour the water away, letting the past and the pain flow away with it.
- Keep the basil leaf or pebble close, as a reminder of your healing.

Full-moon rebirth bath

In witchcraft, the full moon symbolizes strength, transformation and renewal. As the moon reaches its peak, it enhances your connection to your inner wisdom and intuition. This energy bath channels the moon's light to replenish and empower you, fostering deep self-care and belief in yourself.

In this spell, the daisy represents renewal and fresh beginnings while the rosemary promotes cleansing and clarity. Together, these elements help release stagnant energy, allowing new opportunities and growth to flow into your life.

You will need:
- Warm bath or basin of water
- Quiet space under moonlight (or near a window touched by moonlight)
- Single daisy
- Sprig of rosemary
- Pinch of salt

Casting the spell:
- Run your bath or fill a basin with water. If possible, open a window to let the moon's strength fill the room.

- Add the salt, rosemary and daisy to the water, swirling it gently.
- Close your eyes, place your hands on the water and take deep breaths. Visualize the moon's rays infusing your spirit, building your resilience and giving you an entirely fresh phase.
- When finished, let the water drain away. Allow everything that drains you emotionally to go with it.

FOR EXTRA MAGIC:

Use a moon-phase app or calendar to time your bath around the full moon, for maximum effect.

Heart-healing spell

This spell connects you to the sacred act of self-repair, reminding you that even in the broken places, your heart has the strength to mend and love again. Through this ritual, you will embrace the healing process, allowing compassion and patience to flow within. As you perform this spell, feel the gentle energy of love and renewal fill your heart, restoring peace and joy, releasing past hurt and creating safety for new, loving experiences.

You will need:

- Rose quartz
- Silk or cotton cloth, handkerchief or square scarf
- Sprig of rosemary or dried rose petals

Casting the spell:

- Sit in a quiet space you associate with positivity, holding the rose quartz in your palm. Wrap it gently in the cloth with the rosemary or rose petals, creating a "heart bundle".
- Close your eyes and bring the bundle to your chest, over your heart.
- Visualize a golden thread stitching any heartbreak into wholeness, glowing with each stitch.

- Whisper: "Threads of love, weave and mend, let my heart feel whole again."
- Keep the bundle on your altar, under your pillow or carry it with you as a symbol of your ongoing healing journey.

Potion for self-worth

Just a few staples from the pantry can be transformed into something special when you bring intentional focus. This home-made tea is a perfect example of the magic to be harnessed in everyday life. With each ingredient carefully chosen, you invite balance and healing into your life.

In this potion, the camomile is calming and nurturing, cinnamon brings empowerment and passion, and honey releases kindness in yourself. As you sip, feel these qualities infusing your being, elevating your self-worth and nurturing your confidence.

You will need:

- Mug
- Camomile teabag
- Boiling water
- Pinch of ground cinnamon or a single cinnamon stick
- 1 tsp of honey

Brewing the potion:

- Begin by making a mug of camomile tea. Take a deep breath, allowing the aroma to soothe your mind.
- Add a pinch of cinnamon and a teaspoon of honey to the tea. As you stir clockwise, say aloud or silently:

"With each sip, I reclaim my worth, honour my truth and bring love forth."

- As you sip the tea slowly, focus on its warmth filling your body with confidence and a sense of your limitless value.

FOR EXTRA MAGIC:

Stir your potion with a silver spoon, amplifying clarity and intention.

Anointment for kindness

Speaking to yourself kindly is vital for self-love. This ritual will anoint you with an inner monologue based on love and respect.

In this spell, bergamot is for uplifting energy and silencing the inner critic; rose is for self-love, kindness and emotional healing; and lavender is for calmness and releasing negativity. Together, they create a nurturing aura, helping you cultivate a mindset of love and kindness towards yourself and others.

You will need:

- 1 drop of bergamot essential oil
- 1 drop of rose essential oil
- 1 drop of lavender essential oil
- 1½ tbsp of carrier oil (coconut or olive oil will work)
- Small glass bottle or jar

Casting the spell:

- Find a quiet space or go to your altar. Take a few deep breaths to centre yourself.
- To your bottle, add the bergamot, rose and lavender essential oils. Fill the rest of the bottle with your chosen carrier oil, shaking gently to combine the oils.

- Dab the oil blend onto your pulse points – wrists, temples and heart space. As you do this, visualize the oils gently warming your words. Feel any sabotaging self-talk quietening and the voice of love becoming stronger.

LOVE IS YOUR
NATURAL RIGHT

Mirror mantra for body positivity

This refrain is designed to ground you in self-love before your day starts. In a calm space, take deep breaths, inhaling through your nose and exhaling through your mouth to centre yourself.

Gaze gently into a mirror, placing your hand over your heart, and recite:

- "I honour the strength my body gives me."
- "I release society's judgements and embrace myself and my truth."
- "Gratitude fills me for all my body does."
- "I am beautiful, just as I am, inside and out."

Repeat the mantra three times, letting each word affirm your worth and dismantle negativity.

Bibliomancy for self-worth

This ritual harnesses the ancient art of bibliomancy to reflect upon your greatest qualities and confirm your boundless love. Using books to intuit things about yourself is called bibliomancy, and it's a wonderful opportunity to use the words of great writers to slowly build up your own infinite worth.

In this spell, a cherished book serves as a mirror to your spirit, and a herb chosen for clarity and intuition – such as sage or basil – enhances your insight. Together, they affirm your incredible worth and illuminate your path to love.

You will need:

- A treasured book
- Handful of dried sage or basil, crumbled
- Piece of paper
- Pen

Casting the spell:

- Find a quiet space where you feel at peace. When you're ready, open your book to a random page. Without reading the text before you, sprinkle a few fragments of the herbs onto the paper.
- Now look at the words or phrases that the herbs have fallen on or next to. Which resonate with your true self or seem like messages about your qualities?

- Make a note of the words and consider what messages the herbs might be pointing towards. Write down any clarity or inspiration you may have received. Take a moment to let these thoughts settle before resuming your day.

Herbal path spell

This spell focuses on self-love and empowerment, helping you uncover your authentic self. It assists you in shedding limiting beliefs and embracing your full potential. Use it to find and embrace your unique path.

In this spell, bay leaves symbolize clarity and wisdom; rosemary brings protection and strength; lavender promotes calm and intuition; and thyme is for courage and authenticity. Together, these ingredients empower you to stand in your truth, trusting your inner guidance as you move forwards.

You will need:

- Quiet and open outdoor space
- Small bowl of dried herbs:
    - Bay leaves
    - Rosemary
    - Lavender
    - Thyme

Casting the spell:

- Find a peaceful outdoor spot where you can walk and won't be disturbed.
- Hold the bowl of herbs and take five deep breaths to centre yourself. Close your eyes and spend a

few moments in peaceful calm, as you gather your energy and that of the world around you.

- When you feel ready, say: "With each breath, I find my path. With each step, I claim my truth."
- Gently sprinkle the herbs in front of you, forming a trail.
- Slowly walk along the trail you've created. With each step, see yourself walking towards your destiny as your confident true self.

Spells for Finding Love

The universe is always ready to give a little help to those seeking love – especially when you take an active role in your journey towards it. When you bring a focused intention and an open heart, the universe responds in kind. Cast love magic to bring clarity and strength to finding love. Clear lingering blockages in your thinking patterns, amplify your intentions and open your heart to fresh possibilities. Trust that every step you take is leading you towards the love you deserve. This phase is full of possibility and excitement – treat yourself kindly and believe that love is your birthright.

*Love is the most
important thing in life.*

**CHIMAMANDA
NGOZI ADICHIE**

LOVE FINDS THOSE WHO BELIEVE

Love-renewal bath ritual

This simple bathing practice allows you to release old patterns and make space for new, healthy love to come into your life. As you immerse yourself in the soothing waters, feel any stagnant or difficult energy wash away, leaving room for fresh, vibrant love.

In this ritual, the salt is for purification and energetic cleansing, while the lavender is for calming the mind and enhancing emotional healing. Together, these ingredients create a peaceful, transformative experience, helping you reconnect with your heart and open yourself to deeper love and connection.

You will need:

- A bath
- ½ cup of sea salt or pink Himalayan salt
- 3 drops of lavender essential oil

Making the magic:

- In a warm bath, add the salt and a few drops of essential oil. Immerse yourself, close your eyes and visualize the bath washing away pain, regret and toxic patterns from the past.
- As you soak, feel the salt clearing negative energy, and the lavender soothing your heart and mind. Let go of any lingering thoughts or tension in your

body, allowing the water to cleanse and rejuvenate your spirit. When you're ready, step out of the bath, feeling renewed and open to love.

> **FOR EXTRA MAGIC:**
>
> Place a rose quartz near the bath to amplify your emotional healing.

Charm for new beginnings

This charm ritual helps you find new opportunities in love by infusing your thoughts and energy with renewal and joy. By creating this charm, you align yourself with the vibrant possibility of fresh starts and open the door to new, exciting possibilities. This is portable, fragrant and always ready to use, allowing you to have a visible, sensory reminder of what you deserve.

In this ritual, citrine represents positivity and abundance, while cinnamon promotes passion and attraction.

You will need:
- Small pouch or bag
- Citrine
- Cinnamon stick

Making the magic:
- Place the citrine crystal and cinnamon stick into the pouch.
- Hold it in both hands, close your eyes, and focus on inviting loving and joyful energy into your life.
- Tie the pouch securely, setting your intention to welcome new love and fresh connections.
- Keep the charm in your bag, pocket or under your pillow to nurture the energy of new beginnings.

FOR EXTRA MAGIC:

Perform this ritual during a waxing moon, which supports growth and attraction. Carry the charm as a reminder of your openness to love and the opportunities that await. Trust that the energy you've set will guide you towards fulfilling connections.

Magnet-of-love talisman

This magic helps to draw love towards you with the natural power of magnetite. This is a stone celebrated in witchcraft for its magnetic properties and ability to attract what you desire. Historically, magnetite has been used in rituals to enhance manifestation and strengthen intentions. Combined with rose quartz, the stone of unconditional love, and pink cloth to enhance the magic, they become a beacon for the love you seek.

You will need:
- Magnetite
- Rose quartz
- Pink cloth or ribbon

Making the magic:
- Tie the magnetite and rose quartz together with the pink cloth or ribbon. Keep them in your hands and close your eyes.
- Visualize the type of love you wish to attract, focusing on feelings of joy, connection and warmth.
- As you concentrate, feel the stones' energies merging, enhancing your intention to invite loving energy into your life. Take some deep breaths and allow peace, strength and calm to infuse your intention.

- Place the charm close by, perhaps near your bed, on your altar or alternatively carry it with you, to allow its loving magnetic energy to seep into your life.

Love vibration boost

The theory behind vibration is simple: like attracts like. By elevating your own vibration and raising your energy, you emit a frequency that draws in people and experiences that resonate with your desires. This simple practice enhances your energetic presence, making you more attuned to meaningful connections with like-minded people in places right for you. This simple boost raises your cosmic signals to attract connections wherever you go, using amethyst for emotional clarity and to attract positive energy.

You will need:
- Amethyst
- Quiet moment before heading out

Making the magic:
- Hold the amethyst crystal in your hand and close your eyes.
- Take a deep breath and imagine yourself glowing with a soft light that radiates warmth and love.
- See this forming a gentle aura around you, drawing special people into your life.
- Carry the crystal with you in your pocket, bag or as a piece of jewellery.

FOR EXTRA MAGIC:

Each time you go out into the world – whether you're heading out to buy milk, going to work or meeting friends – pause briefly and focus on your boosted vibrations.

Symbolic decluttering spell

For love to find you, sometimes you have to make room for it. This spell releases stagnant energy and will help invite space for new love to enter your life.

In this spell, the white candle symbolizes clarity and new beginnings. Burning sage purifies your environment, removing negative energies, and lavender promotes peace and emotional healing, enhancing your readiness for fresh, loving experiences.

You will need:

- Small paper bag
- Item or piece of paper representing mental clutter you want to clear away
- Pen
- White candle
- Sage or lavender, either herb or incense

Casting the spell:

- In a quiet space where you can focus, light the candle and the cleansing herb or incense.
- Take a few deep breaths, imagining the smoke clearing away old energy.
- Hold the item that is taking up space. Or, write down the things that are taking up too much space and energy in your life on a piece of paper, and hold that instead. Reflect on what you're releasing, be

it heartbreak, limiting beliefs or habits that don't serve you.

- Place the item into the paper bag and set it aside.
- Take a few moments to feel and imagine the space you've created for love.
- Once the ritual feels complete, extinguish the candle and safely dispose of the bag. You might bury it, burn it or throw it away as a final act of release.

Dating-confidence spell

Embarking on the journey of dating can be both exciting and nerve-wracking. To navigate this path with confidence, consider harnessing the transformative power of fire. Fire has long been a symbol of passion, energy and renewal. By connecting with this elemental force, you can ignite your inner strength and embrace new beginnings in your dating life. In this spell, cinnamon is used to promote attraction and courage.

You will need:

- Small fireproof bowl or cauldron
- Piece of paper
- Pen
- Pinch of cinnamon
- Lighter or matches

Casting the spell:

- On the piece of paper, write down the self-doubts or fears holding you back from dating. Be honest and specific – only you will see these.
- Hold the paper over the fireproof bowl. Sprinkle a pinch of cinnamon into the bowl.
- Light the paper with the lighter or matches. As it burns, imagine your fears dissolving into smoke, leaving you lighter and freer.

- Once the paper is completely burned, let the ashes cool and safely discard them outside or in the wind, symbolizing release.

Blessing spell for dating apps

Before dipping your toe into online dating, make your tech a positive portal to love with a simple blessing spell. This spell is designed to infuse your device or app with constructive energy, ensure genuine connections and protect you from negativity, using herbs that will ground and empower you.

In this spell, the bay leaf is for success and blessings; the basil is to bring about protection and luck; the rosemary to promote clarity and focus; and the cinnamon to invoke attraction and warmth.

You will need:
- Bay leaf
- Pinch of basil
- Sprig of rosemary
- Cinnamon stick
- Small pouch or cloth

Casting the spell:
- Lay out the cloth or pouch and place the bay leaf, basil, rosemary and cinnamon in the centre.
- Focus on your intention to attract genuine, positive connections online.
- Tie the pouch securely and wave it gently over your phone or device, imagining it absorbing the positive energies from the herbs.

- Keep the pouch near your phone, laptop or device while using dating apps.

First-date soothing spell

Use the calming and cleansing energy of water to calm your nerves before a date. Water, as a Wiccan element, symbolizes emotions, intuition and healing – perfect for easing those first-night jitters before you head out. The salt is used for grounding, while the mint leaves promote clarity and confidence, and the honey is for sweetness and attraction.

You will need:
- Bowl of water
- Pinch of salt
- Sprig of mint or a few mint leaves
- 1 tsp of honey

Casting the spell:
- Add the salt to your water bowl to create a protective barrier around your emotions.
- Gently stir in the mint leaves. Add the honey to the water for attractive energy in your interactions. Stir clockwise three times.
- Dip your hands into the water and say: "As this water cleanses, I release my nerves and fears."
- Pour the water outdoors onto the earth to dispel your anxiety.

Eloquence spray for conversation

Tongue-tied on the dating scene? This simple spray will help you access the words to make conversation flow and meaningful connections spark. The spray is charged with uplifting energy, symbolizing air (for communication) and joy.

In this potion, the thyme is for courage and clarity; the lemon balm is for joy and positivity; and the orange for attractive energy. Simply spritz, take a deep breath and let your words flow effortlessly.

You will need:

- Small spray bottle
- 1 cup of purified or spring water
- Pinch of thyme
- Pinch of lemon balm
- Small piece of orange peel or 2 drops of orange essential oil
- Honey

Making the magic:

- Boil the water, steeping the thyme and lemon balm in it for 5–10 minutes, like tea. Let it cool and strain out the herbs.

- Add the orange peel (or essential oil) and honey to the cooled water. Stir clockwise while focusing on your intention to speak with confidence, wit and joy.
- Pour the mixture into the spray bottle.
- Before a date, shake the bottle gently and spritz around your throat and heart.

Pendulum dowsing for making choices

Making decisions, especially in matters of the heart, can be overwhelming. Doubts creep in and it's easy to second-guess yourself. But you don't have to navigate these choices alone. The universe holds endless wisdom and a pendulum acts as a portal to that. A pendulum is a small, weighted object suspended from a chain or string that taps into subconscious energy. It can help guide you towards better choices in dating and relationships, and is a powerful tool for those seeking clarity in their love life.

Make one by tying a crystal or household key to a string or chain.

Using the pendulum:
- Hold it steady and ask test questions to determine its movements for "yes", "no" and "maybe".
- Once calibrated, ask specific love-related questions, such as: "Is this person a good match for me?" or "Will this relationship bring long-term happiness?"
- If on a dating app, hold your pendulum over your phone and ask: "Is this person right for me?" to help you decide whether to swipe right for yes.

FOR EXTRA MAGIC:

Cleanse your pendulum before using, either mentally or with a sage-burn. Choose your crystal carefully – rose quartz is associated with love, while clear quartz is good for focus and clarity.

Spells for True Love

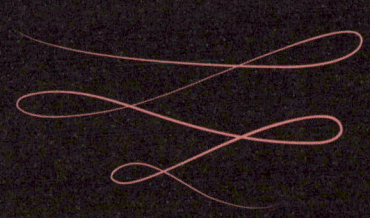

Love is a force as ancient and boundless as the stars, but even the strongest flames need tending. When love finds you, it requires care, intention and a touch of magic to thrive. Sometimes, emotions fade, connections waver or new love feels just out of reach. But with the right energy, you can nurture passion, strengthen bonds and awaken feelings long forgotten. Whether you're seeking to deepen a relationship, attract romance or rekindle lost sparks, these love spells, potions and rituals will amplify the magic that is within you and use it to forge meaningful partnerships.

*If you pay close attention to each day,
you will discover the magic moment.*

PAULO COELHO

CHOOSE LOVE
DAILY AND
MIRACLES WILL
HAPPEN

Love passion potion

This enchanting aphrodisiac is designed to awaken the senses, deepen intimacy and enhance attraction. Inspired by ancient traditions, each ingredient carries symbolic and energetic properties to ignite the passion and warmth between you and a potential partner.

In this potion, pomegranate is a fruit long associated with love, fertility and sensuality; honey symbolizes the sweetness of love; cinnamon is for desire and energy; cayenne is a fiery spice that awakens the senses and sparks passion; and rose represents love, romance and beauty.

You will need:

- 1 cup of pomegranate juice
- 1 tbsp of honey
- 1 tsp of cinnamon
- Pinch of cayenne
- 3 rose petals
- Saucepan
- Cup

Brewing the potion:

- In a small saucepan, gently heat the pomegranate juice.
- In a clockwise motion, stir in the honey, cinnamon and cayenne, allowing the flavours to blend.

- Once warmed, remove from the heat and add the rose petals. Let the mixture steep for 5 minutes, then strain into a cup.
- Share this elixir with your partner and set your intentions for connection.

Love cleanse

This powerful ritual helps clear emotional baggage and past hurts, whether recent or long held, to create space for love and harmony. Releasing negativity allows positive energy to flow freely, helping love flourish. Clear quartz and sunstone bring light and optimism, while salt provides protection and purification. Lavender and sage remove lingering negative energy, restoring peace and emotional balance. This cleanse is perfect for renewing your heart, strengthening relationships and welcoming love with an open spirit.

You will need:

- Clear quartz or sunstone
- Small bowl
- A pinch of salt
- Sprig of lavender or a few sticks of sage incense

Making the magic:

- Sit in a quiet space with your partner and take turns to hold the clear quartz or sunstone between your hands.
- Take turns sprinkling a pinch of salt into the bowl, mentally releasing any lingering negativity.
- Pass the lavender or incense around each other in circular motions, visualizing dark energy dissolving.

- Place the stone in your shared space as a symbol of light, protection and renewal.

Knot of devotion spell

Got a knotty problem? Untangle things with this simple but meaningful spell. It weaves a powerful bond between you and your partner, creating a tangible symbol of your love, promises and shared desires. As you tie each knot, you reinforce your connection and set clear intentions for your future together. Every knot represents a promise, a wish or a heartfelt intention, drawing you closer. This ritual deepens trust, fosters understanding and reminds you both of the love and unity you share. Embrace the magic of connection and let love grow stronger.

You will need:
- Red ribbon or cord
- Piece of paper
- Pen

Casting the spell:
- Together, write down three things you cherish most about each other, followed by three wishes for your relationship. This could be plans for the future or things you'd like to change.
- Speak them aloud to each other, and talk them through if you want, or just allow them to seep into the air around you. Make a promise to listen without judgement or response. This is about speaking aloud and letting the words seep in.

- For each agreed wish or promise, tie a knot in the ribbon, imbuing it with intention and love.
- Keep the ribbon as a token of your sacred bond.

Kind conversation spell

Since ancient times, honey has been used in magic and ritual. In witchcraft, it is often employed in honey jars to sweeten relationships, mend broken bonds and encourage kind-hearted speech. Honey brings sweetness; the feather, representing air, brings wisdom; while herbs will lend their calm for constructive conversations that deepen your love. This spell helps soothe tensions, promote understanding and open hearts to compassionate dialogue. Whether healing past wounds or simply strengthening your bond, this gentle ritual fosters patience, empathy and warmth.

You will need:

- 1 tsp of honey
- Feather
- Candle, any colour
- Sprig of lavender or rosemary

Casting the spell:

- Sit facing each other and place the feather between you.
- Light the candle to set an atmosphere of calm and understanding, and focus your thoughts and energy towards each other.
- Pass the spoon of honey between you and each have a taste.

- When you feel calm and ready to speak, begin. Pass the feather to each other as you take turns talking, ensuring voices remain calm and loving.
- Once finished, place the feather and herb in a meaningful place as a symbol of harmony in communication.
- Blow out the candle together, sealing the intention of peace.

Shield spell

Love is a living force, resilient and ever-growing. Yet over time, even the strongest bonds face storms, such as illness, conflict or external pressures. This ritual actively weaves a shield of protection around your relationship, calling upon the elements to strengthen and reinforce your love.

In this spell, black tourmaline and amethyst represent protection and strength; moon-charged water promotes emotional clarity; sea salt is used for purification and resilience; and the branch or leaf symbolizes growth and endurance.

You will need:
- Black tourmaline or amethyst
- Bowl of moon-charged water
- Pinch of sea salt
- Small branch or leaf

Casting the spell:
- Stand together, holding the stone between you. Close your eyes and take deep, steady breaths in sync.
- Stir the salt into the water with the branch or leaf, saying: "We stand strong, protected by love."

- Dip your fingers in the water and trace a protective circle around each other.
- Bury the branch or leaf near the entrance to your home to ground your love in strength and harmony.

Fidelity charm

Crystals have long been revered for their ability to channel energy and intention. Rose quartz – the stone of love – encourages deep, unwavering commitment, while amethyst offers protection to guard against external temptation. A silver coin represents steadfast loyalty, holding the value of lasting faith in your bond. Carry this charm with you to deepen your bond, creating a sense of security and protection against negativity. As its energy surrounds you, let it nurture honesty, ignite passion and keep your love unwavering through every challenge.

You will need:

- Small pouch
- Piece of rose quartz or amethyst
- Silver coin

Casting the spell:

- Hold the crystal in your dominant hand and the silver coin in the other, feeling their energies connect.
- Close your eyes and visualize a protective shield around you and your partner, strengthening your bond and repelling negativity.
- Focus on your love, trust and the commitment you share.

- When you're ready, place all the items into your pouch, sealing them with your heartfelt intention.
- Carry the charm with you as a constant reminder of your loyalty and devotion. Whenever doubts arise, hold it close, breathe deeply and reaffirm your promise to remain faithful, strong and true.

Next-step spell

If you're ready to take things to the next level, this spell – performed under the open sky – can help you break through stagnation and guide a relationship to its next chapter. This ritual clears doubts, strengthens commitment and paves the way for deeper connection. Embrace the energy, trust in the journey and let the process illuminate the path forwards.

In this spell, bay leaves are for wisdom and decision-making; rose petals are for deepened romance; and orange peel is for joy and movement.

You will need:

- Small bonfire or firepit
- Piece of paper
- Pen
- Handful of bay leaves
- Handful of rose petals
- Peel of an orange
- Small jar or pouch

Casting the spell:

- Sit by the lit fire, holding hands with your partner. Take a deep breath and speak your desire to move forwards, whether by deepening commitment, moving in together or overcoming hesitation. Write this down.

- Toss the bay leaves, rose petals and orange peel into the flames, imagining the heat sparking your path forwards
- Read your commitment aloud, then place the paper in the fire
- Once cooled, collect some ash in a jar or pouch as a keepsake and reminder of the love and commitment you've set in motion.

Weekend reset spell

If you've had a long week but want to enjoy a love-filled weekend with your partner, this spell is for you. Friday, ruled by Venus, is the perfect time for love spells. This nourishing bath helps you and your partner cleanse away the week's stress and set a magical tone for the weekend ahead.

In this spell, lavender is for peace, relaxation and harmony, while rose is for love and beauty.

You will need:

- 3 drops of lavender essential oil or a handful of dried lavender
- Handful of rose petals
- Small token, such as a charm, shell or stone
- Bath

Casting the spell:

- Run a warm bath for you and your partner, adding the lavender oil or dried lavender and rose petals. As you both settle into the water, close your eyes and breathe deeply. Let the lavender's calming energy soothe you. Hold your token together, charging it with the bath's peaceful energy, saying together: "In this token, our love will stay, To guide us through this weekend's way."

- Keep the token close throughout the weekend as a reminder of the loving energy you've created.

Scrying spell for guidance

Scrying is a form of divination where you observe patterns in reflective surfaces or scattered items, such as herbs or petals, to gain insights. This not only strengthens intuition but will also deepen your connection, allowing you to see beyond words, and to gain insights into each other's thinking patterns and clarity on enhancing your relationship.

In this spell, lavender is for peace, rosemary is for love and thyme is for strength.

You will need:
- Handful of dried herbs like lavender, rosemary or thyme
- Bowl of water
- Quiet, comfortable space

Casting the spell:
- Gently scatter the herbs over the water.
- Hold hands, breathe deeply and focus on your connection. Ask: "What can we do to strengthen our love and connection?" or other questions that feel right.
- Watch how the herbs settle and form patterns. You may notice shapes – such as a heart or bridge (which could mean healing and new beginnings) or key (which could represent unlocking something

important) – that could offer insights into your relationship. Trust your intuition to guide you towards these.

- Discuss the patterns and what they reveal about your relationship.
- Thank the universe and pour the water away mindfully.

Gratitude spell

Sometimes, we fail to see our partner properly. Habit, work and stress can cloud our perception and render important things invisible. This spell clears your vision, revealing your partner's hidden strengths and helping to rekindle deep appreciation, ensuring you won't take them for granted.

In this spell, the mirror is for reflecting unseen strengths; the white/gold candle is for clarity; the rosemary is for insight; and the clear quartz is for perception and awareness.

You will need:

- Small mirror
- White or gold candle
- Sprig of rosemary
- Piece of paper
- Pen
- Clear quartz

Casting the spell:

- Light the candle and place the mirror before it so the flame reflects. Hold the rosemary in one hand and the paper in the other.
- Write your partner's name at the top of the paper, followed by three things you cherish about them. Leave space for more.
- Look into the mirror and whisper: "Show me strengths I fail to see, so gratitude may set us free."

- Hold the quartz, feeling it awaken your awareness. Write down three hidden strengths you now perceive.
- Extinguish the candle. Place the rosemary under your pillow to help bring dreams of your partner's gifts.

Spells for Friendship

Friendship is love – pure and simple. It's the kind of love that holds you up, makes you laugh and walks with you through life's ups and downs. But even the most meaningful friendships need a little TLC from time to time. Whether you want to grow closer with the friends you already have, make tough decisions together or heal any emotional bumps along the way, magic can help. This chapter will give you the tools to strengthen those bonds, bring understanding and attract new friendships that feel like home. With love and intention, you'll nurture connections that truly last.

Squad loyalty spell

Friendship is a rare and sacred bond that is strengthened through coming together and expressing your love for each other. This spell calls upon the power of unity and seals your friendship group's connection with love and a joyous celebration.

In this spell, the yellow, orange or gold candle promotes warmth and unity.

You will need:
- Ribbons in different colours, one for each friend
- Large yellow, orange or gold candle
- Shared meal or drink for the group
- Musical instruments or your favourite playlist

Casting the spell:
- Gather in a circle with all friends present. Light the candle and let its flame symbolize the strength of your bond.
- Invite each friend to voice what they cherish about the group while taking it in turns to tie their ribbon to the ribbon that has gone before. By the end, all the ribbons should be tied together.
- When the collective knot is complete, each friend

places their hand on it and voices their loyalty, in their own words.

- Celebrate with food, drink, music or all three, to honour your friendship and seal your bond. Let the knot pass from friend to friend through the year. When it has become frayed, consider holding a renewal gathering.

Magnet spell

There's an entire world out there that hums with unseen threads of connection, waiting to bring new friendships into your life. This attraction spell for new platonic relationships opens your heart, brightens your energy and beckons kindred spirits to your side.

In this spell, the citrine or sunstone helps you to shine with confidence and charm, the lavender attracts kind souls, the cinnamon or clove sparks lively connections and the feather helps to carry your intentions on the wind.

You will need:

- Citrine or sunstone
- Sprig of lavender
- Pinch of cinnamon or a clove
- Feather
- Small sachet or charm bag
- Piece of paper
- Pen

Casting the spell:

- Take the paper and pen, and write your intention to bring new friends into your life, in your own words. Be as descriptive as possible, as this is a safe space. Be fearless in your request. What qualities do you want your friends to have? How do you want them to show up for you?

- Place the lavender, cinnamon, crystal and feather into the sachet.
- Carry the charm with you, especially when you go out. Place it nearby when you are using a friendship app or digital meetup group, as a reminder of your needs and what you truly seek.

Connection potion

In Wiccan tradition, potions are more than simple brews – they are vessels of intent. This potion strengthens your aura to make you a beacon for kindred spirits. As you drink, feel yourself align with the energy of connection, allowing new friendships to manifest with ease.

In this potion, basil is for harmony and attracting positive relationships; rose petals are used to invite loving, genuine connections; camomile promotes warmth, peace and effortless conversations; and cinnamon is for sparking exciting new friendships.

You will need:
- Handful of fresh basil leaves
- Handful of dried rose petals
- Camomile teabag
- Pinch of cinnamon
- Mug
- Boiling water

Brewing the potion:
- Steep the basil, rose petals, cinnamon and camomile teabag in boiling water for 5–10 minutes, allowing their energies to blend and infuse the water with warmth and intention.
- As the fragrant steam rises, take a moment to breathe deeply and centre yourself in the moment.

- Strain, then hold the cup in both hands. As you sip, close your eyes and visualize new friendships effortlessly blossoming in your life – connections filled with joy, trust and mutual understanding.
- Let each sip welcome positive energy and meaningful relationships into your world.

Your friend is your needs answered.

KAHLIL GIBRAN

FRIENDSHIP IS
A SPELL CAST BY
THE HEART

Scrying spell for decisions

Not all friendships are meant to last forever – some teach us lessons in the moment, while others grow with us. If you're unsure whether to nurture or release a connection, this spell will reveal the truth and help you decide where to invest your energy.

In this spell, the black candle symbolizes protection and insight; the mirror, water or crystal ball are used for divination; the amethyst is to promote wisdom and intuition; and the lavender is intended to bring about calm and clarity.

You will need:

- Black candle
- Clear mirror, bowl of water or crystal ball
- Amethyst
- 3–4 drops of lavender oil
- Piece of paper
- Pen

Casting the spell:

- Light the black candle and anoint the mirror (or water/crystal ball) with lavender oil while focusing on your question. Let the calming scent relax your mind and open your intuition.
- Write the question about your friendship on the paper and place it beneath the mirror or near the crystal.

- Take a deep breath, clearing your thoughts, and centre yourself in the moment.
- Gaze softly into the reflective surface, allowing images, symbols or emotions to guide you.
- Trust your intuition – your answer will reveal itself, offering clarity, wisdom and insight.

Charm to forgive

Friendship, like all relationships, can go through difficult patches. These are best addressed if you want to strengthen the bond. So, when hurt lingers, this charm helps dissolve tension, mend the relationship and invite peace, in a non-confrontational way. Forgiveness is not just for others – it frees your own heart, too.

In this charm, lavender acts to soothe emotions and encourage reconciliation; rosemary promotes healing and clarity; and the mirror helps to reflect understanding and release negativity.

You will need:

- 2 sprigs of lavender
- Sprig of rosemary
- Clean cloth
- Small mirror
- Piece of paper
- Pen
- Candle, any colour

Making the magic:

- Write the conflict or hurt feelings on the paper with honesty and clarity. Place it under the mirror, symbolizing deep self-reflection and resolution. Gently crush the herbs together in your hands to release their aroma. Take some breaths in.

- Light a candle and focus on healing energy as you safely burn the paper, releasing past pain and negativity into the universe.
- Gaze into the mirror and picture both you and your friend at peace, rekindling understanding and warmth. If you feel able, say a few kind words to your friend as if he or she were there.
- When you feel ready, wipe the mirror with the cloth as a symbol of a true fresh start.

A spell to reach out

This spell calls upon the element of air – the force of connection – to carry help and love to a friend in need. It is best performed somewhere open and peaceful – a hill overlooking rolling fields, beneath an ancient tree or by a quiet stream – where the breeze can take your words to those who need them.

In this spell, the white candle brings light and comfort and the rose quartz radiates love and connection. May the winds and the natural world quicken healing and may your friend find what they are looking for.

You will need:

- Quiet outdoor spot
- White candle
- Rose quartz
- Piece of paper
- Pen
- Lighter or matches

Casting the spell:

- Find a quiet outdoor spot where the air is stirring gently. Light the white candle.
- Write your friend's name and a few words of comfort on the paper.
- Hold the rose quartz in your hands, filling it with love. Picture your friend surrounded by light, warmth, blessings and companionship.

- Burn the paper safely, then scatter the cooled ashes into the wind, trusting the air to carry your wish.

FOR EXTRA MAGIC:

Give the rose quartz to your friend or place it somewhere meaningful, letting the spell continue its quiet work.

Banishing jealousy spell

It's normal, from time to time, for jealousy to creep into friendships. This spell calls upon the grounding power of earth to acknowledge and dissolve envy, and restore harmony. It is best performed in a quiet place where you feel safe and centred.

In this spell, bay leaves are used for protection and to banish negativity; salt is for purification and protection; and amethyst promotes calm and understanding. Together they will work to root out jealousy, replacing it with trust, balance and the deep strength of true friendship.

You will need:

- Small fireproof dish
- Dried bay leaf
- Pinch of salt
- Amethyst
- Lighter or matches

Casting the spell:

- Place the amethyst nearby. Hold the bay leaf and focus on any jealousy or tension, visualizing it dissolving into nothingness. Then set it alight in the fireproof dish, watching the smoke carry the negativity away into the universe, leaving only peace and acceptance.

- Sprinkle salt around the dish, forming a protective barrier against any lingering envy. This will seal your intention for harmony and renewed friendship.
- Sit for a moment in gratitude, picturing your friendship strengthened and free from resentment.
- Once the ashes have cooled, scatter them outside, letting the earth absorb and transform the energy.

Smudge stick for entertaining

A smudge stick is a bundle of herbs, often tied with string, used in witchcraft to purify a space, object or person. Smudging clears negative energy and invites positive vibrations, and is often done before significant events to create positivity. This smudge stick contains cherry to promote love and friendship, rosemary for warmth and protection, and thyme for strengthening bonds. When lit, the smoke clears unwanted energy, filling the space with peace, love and harmony. This spell will ensure a warm, welcoming environment for social activity.

You will need:

- 3 cherry incense sticks
- Large bunch of dried rosemary stems
- Large bunch of dried thyme sprigs
- Thread, to tie the herbs

Casting the spell:

- Only dried herbs will burn cleanly, so make sure your herbs are extremely dry. If in doubt, put them in the oven for 10 minutes at a low heat.
- Tie the dried herbs tightly with the thread.
- Light the smudge stick and let it smoulder. If there are flames, shake the stick to extinguish them.

- Walk around your house or space with intention. Waft the smoke around each room, allowing its fragrance to fill your space, before moving on.
- Extinguish the smudge stick safely and then open a window to welcome fresh energy.

Gossip-healing spell

Is your friendship group going through a tricky patch? This spell calls upon the grounding power of garlic and the healing energy of amber to dispel gossip and restore harmony.

In this spell, amber is used to promote truth and resolution; garlic offers protection against gossip; water is for cleansing and to reset energy; and the yellow or orange candle brings clarity.

You will need:
- Yellow or orange candle
- Amber
- Clove of garlic
- Bowl of water
- Piece of paper
- Pen

Casting the spell:
- Light the candle and hold the amber and garlic, imagining them glowing with protective energy.
- Write your concerns on the piece of paper, read them aloud, then tear the paper into small pieces. Drop them into the water, stirring gently in an anticlockwise direction to dispel negativity and let it dissolve.
- Whisper: "Amber mends and garlic defends, let truth be spoken, trust transcend."

- Dip the garlic into the water and place it by your door. Keep the amber close.
- Blow out the candle and discard the water outdoors, letting the earth transform negativity into peace.

Get-together go-getter spell

This spell calls upon the warmth of fire and the clarity of air to bring you self-assurance, renew old bonds and welcome joy into your heart. Best performed before stepping into a reunion, or any gathering of friends where you want to shine brightly.

In this spell, the gold or white candle represents confidence and new beginnings, the rosemary promotes clarity, self-trust and the strengthening of old connections, while the mirror is used to reflect your true and radiant self.

You will need:
- Small gold or white candle
- Sprig of rosemary
- Mirror

Casting the spell:
- Light the candle and hold the rosemary, inhaling its uplifting scent.
- Stand before the mirror and gaze at your reflection – not just at your appearance, but at the love, strength and warmth you carry within.
- Repeat:

    "I am welcomed, I am loved, I shine as I am.
    The past is well, the future bright,
    With love and joy, my heart is light."

- Pass the rosemary through the candle's flame, sealing your intention.
- Blow out the candle, feeling the light within you continue to glow.

Conclusion

As you close the pages of this book, know that the power to manifest love is now within you. The spells you've discovered are not just words or rituals, but keys to unlocking the deepest desires of your heart and putting them into words. This, in itself, carries great transformative power.

Remember, love is not a destination but a journey – one that begins with self-awareness, intention and trust in the universe. Acknowledging that you deserve it must be at the forefront of your mind at all times.

May your path be illuminated with warmth, laughter and the pure joy of connection. May you find love in unexpected places. May it fill your life with endless possibilities. But above all, may you always return to the most important love there will ever be – the love within yourself.

As you move forwards, check in with your own needs regularly; the foundation of any lasting bond is the strength and balance you cultivate within. The energy you send out will always return to you – so send it with intent, clarity and an open heart. To remind yourself of your love magic tools, dip into this book often, and consider writing an accompanying journal to record your progress and remember what you want to nourish in your life.

The magic is in your hands. With every spell cast, remember that you are the creator of your own story.

Let love guide you.

Notes

HERBAL MAGIC

Lydia Levine

Hardback

978-1-83799-129-7

Step into the enchanting world of herbal recipes, remedies and rituals with this spellbinding guide to the magical power of plants

Including a variety of crafts, spells and rituals, this treasury of herb profiles is the perfect introduction to conjuring your inner power and enriching your life with a little herbal magic. Whether you are drawn to blends and brews or elixirs and potions, the unique natural powers of these bewitching ingredients are ready and waiting for you.

Have you enjoyed this book? If so, find us on Facebook at **Summersdale Publishers**, on Twitter/X at **@Summersdale** and on Instagram, TikTok and Bluesky at **@summersdalebooks** and get in touch. We'd love to hear from you!

www.summersdale.com

Image credits

Cover art by Marianne Thompson; pp.3, 4–5, 14–15, 28–29, 40–41, 50–51, 154–158 – toadstool and plants © Mio Buono/Shutterstock.com; pp.12–13, 24–25, 38–39, 48–49 – plants © Mio Buono/Shutterstock.com, feathers © ne2pi/Shutterstock.com, potions © renberry/Shutterstock.com, bird © Martyshova Maria/Shutterstock.com; p.61 – blue candle © Mito Photography/Shutterstock.com; p.63 – salt, rosemary and lavender © Cora Mueller/Shutterstock.com; p.65 – pebbles and candles © Subbotina Anna/Shutterstock.com; p.67 – window view of a night sky © Athapet Piruska/Shutterstock.com; p.69 – rose quartz © Kellymmiller73/Shutterstock.com; p.71 – camomile tea © Es75/Shutterstock.com; p.73 – essential oils © Vera Prokhorova/Shutterstock.com; p.77 – stack of antique books © LN team/Shutterstock.com; p.79 – bowl of dried herbs © barmalini/Shutterstock.com; p.85 – bath with lavender and pink Himalayan salt © Tatyana Soares/Shutterstock.com; pp.87, 133 – citrine crystals © eloresnorwood/Shutterstock.com; p.89 – magnetite © mineral vision/Shutterstock.com; p.91 – amethyst © Nina Stankevicha/Shutterstock.com; p.93 – white candles and lavender © mama_mia/Shutterstock.com; p.95 – burning paper © Josu Ozkaritz/Shutterstock.com; p.97 – small pouch © liev.mark/Shutterstock.com; p.99 – mint leaves in water © ZCOOL HelloRF/Shutterstock.com; p.101 – spray bottle and orange peel © Switlana S/Shutterstock.com; p.103 – amethyst pendulum © FotoHelin/Shutterstock.com; p.109 – pomegranate juice © Sergii Koval/Shutterstock.com; p.111 – quartz © Rido/Shutterstock.com; p.113 – red ribbons © caimacanul/Shutterstock.com; p.115 – candle, feather and cauldron © Doris Assenheimer/Shutterstock.com; p.119 – amethyst © ju_see/Shutterstock.com; p.121 – fire © Igor Link/Shutterstock.com; p.123 – lavender essential oils © Madeleine Steinbach/Shutterstock.com; p.125 – bowl of herbs in water © symbiot/Shutterstock.com; p.127 – candle in mirror © Hissiyat Gezgini/Shutterstock.com; p.131 – coloured ribbons © pote-poteco/Shutterstock.com; p.135 – camomile tea and rose petals © Peiling Lee/Shutterstock.com; p.139 – crystal ball © ju_see/Shutterstock.com; p.141 – lavender and notebook © Irina Bort/Shutterstock.com; p.143 – stack of rose quartz © CoralAntler/Shutterstock.com; p.145 – burning bay leaves © banu sevim/Shutterstock.com; p.147 – smudge stick © Microgen/Shutterstock.com; p.149 – orange candle © Olinda Gonsalves/Shutterstock.com; p.151 – rosemary © Fantiki photo/Shutterstock.com; p.177 – black tourmaline and amethyst © Holly Mazour/Shutterstock.com